Highs and Lows

A Collection of Life Stories Written by Teens and Young Adults on the Path to Recovery

D1457928

"Your highs will be higher. The lows will be lower. If you think your heart can take it, come fly with us."

To my loving parents:
Toma and Andrew Wolff

Mom and Dad,

You have always stood by my side, through the good times and definitely through the bad times as well, whether I wanted it or not. You have been through hell and back with me, and by some crazy miracle, we ended up on the other side. You introduced me to hope and then allowed my recovery to do the rest. I don't want you to think I'm "fixed", but because of the two of you, I'm a lot better than I was.

Love you Mom and Dad.

Your son,

Simon Wolff

Thank you to Charlotte Matthews who contributed her time and talents to illustrate the cover artwork.

H&L

CONTENTS

FORWARD   i

A BETTER WAY   1

A DARK PATH   9

INTERNAL ANNIHILATION   16

BY THE GRACE OF GOD   29

I'LL BE HAPPY WHEN   35

JUST ONE FRIEND   47

VISIONS & VOICES   52

FALLING SHORT   65

LEAP OF FAITH   71

PART OF A PACK   74

DOPE HOUSE   78

A CROOKED PICTURE   82

SAD, STUCK, AND SICK   87

BROKEN GLASS EVERYWHERE: A
COUNTER-CULTURAL DILEMMA   93

RESOURCES   104

H&L

FORWARD

By Simon Wolff

Two and a half years have passed since I entered recovery. I was lucky enough to be initiated into a program with a large support group that helped me and loved me through all my hardships, as well as my successes. At least for me, it was imperative to my success to be able to relate to someone who understood my struggles and had dealt with problems and situations similar to my own. But I didn't always have people with whom I could relate, whose life experiences were like my own.

When I first entered recovery, I read many books focused on drug addiction and alcoholism, but none spoke to me in particular. I've seen firsthand how people find great faith, guidance, and hope from self-help books, and it made me wonder why young people's recovery did not have the same resources. I knew I couldn't be the only one craving this: a connection to someone who understands my life, how my head works. This is when I decided to take matters into my own hands and compile my own version of a recovery book for young people.

The overall concept of this book was spawned during a time when I was in an intensive inpatient program in Arizona. Every morning and night, we would do an activity called "highs and lows". During this time, each of us would share our cool and bad experiences throughout our day. As insignificant as this activity may seem, it was actually a very beneficial indicator of my progress while in treatment. Slowly but surely, my extensive list of "lows" and sparse list of "highs" transformed into more "highs" than "lows". Those 45 days spent in the desert would quickly change my life and allow me to turn things around. I thought that if I created a book with this concept, maybe it would benefit others and give them hope.

So, I set out to collect personal stories from young people in recovery. But it wasn't easy. I contacted local free and for-profit recovery programs, only to be shut down. Next, I researched university recovery programs across the nation. I sent countless emails and made numerous phone calls to directors of the programs. I sent out a questionnaire for my book, *Highs and Lows*, hoping that simply filling in some blanks would encourage more participants. Some were receptive and others were not. I hosted several get-togethers with peers from my own recovery community, explaining my goal and asking for help. At times, I questioned whether this work was worth it. Eventually, the support for my book started to trickle - and then pour - in.

I have self-published the first edition of my book dedicated to young people's recovery. *Highs and Lows: A Collection of Personal Stories Written by Teens and Young Adults on the Path to Recovery* is for sale on Amazon. To further help others like myself, all proceeds from book sales will be donated to Love Enough 4 U (www.loveenough4u.org) a foundation established to help young people with the expenses of private recovery programs.

I am excited to share these stories and be a force for positive growth. My hope is that this book will also reach people not in recovery, so that they will appreciate our similarities and not focus on our differences. I think that people automatically search for what separates us from others, rather than looking for what we have in common. This natural response pushes people away from each other instead of joining together to make each other stronger.

My dream is that this book helps young people everywhere – those in need of recovery, educational resources, and a safe, welcoming group where, ultimately, they can share their own story.

"We are people who normally would not mix. But there exists among us a fellowship, friendliness, and an understanding which is indescribably wonderful." Anonymous

H&L

A BETTER WAY OF LIFE

By Corina

Early childhood:

I grew up in a house with my mother and father and two older brothers. On the surface it seemed like a happy family. I remember from a young age, I feared a lot of things. I was raised Christian and was always worried that if I didn't have God in my life I was doomed to hell. I would quickly get obsessed with things I enjoyed. I played a lot of sports. I did have a few friends. My brothers excluded me a lot; they were closer in age and older. They didn't want to spend a lot of time with me. When I went to private school, my friends didn't treat me very well. They would insult me and get me to do things that would embarrass me. Going into fifth grade I went to public school. I started having a lot of anger issues. I remember not feeling very happy with myself. I was aggressive toward other people and would hurt them physically and emotionally. I got my first boyfriend, and it ended on bad terms. He and his friends would follow me home and throw rocks at me. I would sit alone at lunch. I had maybe one friend at this point. After that happened, I started cutting myself. Not too much, just a little bit. That was the beginning.

Middle school:

The summer before 7th grade was when I first tried drugs. My brother always talked about how amazing smoking weed was. I wanted to feel better than I did, so I thought anything was worth a shot. The first time I smoked weed, I didn't get high, but I wanted to try again. The end of summer I smoked again, and it was life changing. I loved smoking weed; it fixed all my problems. The same was true with drinking. I started drinking consistently only a couple months after smoking weed. I wanted to be high or under the influence all the time. I didn't have to feel unhappy with myself or think about my insecurities. I started dressing more revealing and loved getting attention. I felt more confident and thought people liked me more when I was high or under the influence. Being a drug user became my reputation in middle school.

I was cutting a lot at this point because I didn't know how to cope with my anger. At the same time, my brother was getting into lot of legal trouble. He was going downhill quickly. I wanted to be like him. Doing bad things was appealing to me. I would get high with my brother and cousin fairly consistently. I didn't have many other friends. I preferred keeping one friend at a time. I started getting bullied by kids at school again. They would take my journals from me and read them out loud to people at lunch. I got sexually harassed and called names in the hallways. I would go to the bathroom to be alone. I went to the nurses' office almost every day. I'd go in there and say that I wasn't feeling well, and they knew I was on something. They would call my mom to come get me. I was prescribed Adderall and antidepressants for my depression/anxiety and ADHD. I would abuse my Adderall. My classmates would tell the counselor I was cutting myself. The counselor would ask me why I was cutting myself, and I didn't know why. I just became addicted to it. I didn't feel much at this point. I wanted to feel something. I picked up the habit of stealing. I'd steal money and alcohol from my friends, their parents, and stores at the mall.

My parents were having a lot of trouble too. I started noticing that they didn't agree on a lot of things. My dad had drug and drinking issues. My dad was unhappy, emotionally unstable, and acting like a fool, and he was around less and less. My mom was always dealing with my brother's drug problems. It was so easy for me to get away with things because she was so focused on him. I would leave the house in the middle of the night without anyone knowing.

I got caught with weed in 7th grade at school. I didn't get into any legal trouble because my friend flushed it down the toilet. I remember coming home expecting to get in a lot of trouble. My parents were both disappointed but didn't yell at me. I remember thinking: if that were the worst trouble I would get into, than it's not too bad. My friend's mom met with my mom and told her I needed help and that I was a troublemaker. I lost that friend. I made another friend who was always mad at me because I was always under the influence. I stopped hanging out with her. I introduced any new friends that I made into drugs and my drug lifestyle. I had poor body image. I was always worried about being fat, so I would eat sparingly and some days I would not eat at all. I would burn myself in addition to cutting myself. One time my mom caught me cutting myself in the bathroom. My mom lifted up my sleeves and was upset. She asked me to stop and wanted to know why I was hurting myself. I had zero emotional reaction to that.

The summer before 8th grade, I continued down that same path. My brother went into jail and then went into drug treatment. Once he got out, he joined Full Circle, a program for at-risk youths, most of whom had drug/alcohol issues. I decided to join Full Circle also. I met some people there and started getting high with them. I put myself in bad circumstances with guys. I was in therapy at the time. I didn't enjoy therapy, and I ran away from my therapist once. I didn't like talking to a cheerful person when I was depressed. My parents were close to getting a divorce at this time; they fought all the time. My dad would lean on me for emotional support. I would lock myself in my mom's room to keep away from my dad. I was sent to my grandparents' house for about a month to get away from him. I debated running away a lot.

At the end of eighth grade, I took a couple Vicodin and drank a bottle of whiskey and went to school impaired. I overdosed in the bathroom and was taken out on a stretcher. I went to Marillac because I was suicidal and told the paramedics I wanted to die. At Marillac, I was withdrawing off alcohol. I was very irritable. When I got out I planned on continuing to live the same way, using drugs and alcohol.

Sobriety:

My mom told me I needed to find somewhere to go get help. She gave me a few options, and one of them was Crossroads, an outpatient program for teens and young adults with drug and alcohol addictions. I met with the Crossroads counselors. They didn't know if they could help me because the overdose was ruled a suicide attempt, but I ended up joining Crossroads for outpatient treatment when I was 14 years old.

After a couple weeks of treatment, I realized the people there had found a better way of life. I wanted a second chance to have a better way of living, like they had. At first, it was hard for me to change my way of life. I would still hook up with guys, steal, and talk to old friends. I relapsed in outpatient after two months of sobriety. I realized that my way of life didn't work, and that I needed to change things in order to be happy. I gave my phone to my sponsor, and she removed social media and closed my back doors to getting high. I started working the steps and stopped hanging out with people who weren't good for me. I lied a lot in outpatient, but after some time, I realized that the people in treatment with me would love me regardless. I didn't need to lie about who I was.

After getting some time sober, it was time for me to give back what I received. When I got my year sober, I realized I am capable of anything I set my mind to. This was my biggest life accomplishment. I've never felt so free and fulfilled as I do in my sobriety. I now have a great relationship with my family. I sponsor someone who is so much like me. The biggest lesson I've learned through sobriety is that we rise by lifting others. I know that I'm not held back from my past and that I never have to feel alone ever again. At different times I wanted to give up, but I kept hope. This was the best decision I've ever made. Through my sobriety there have been many ups and downs, but I know that I don't need drugs, alcohol, or a guy to get me through it. I just need to keep walking through my fears even though it's uncomfortable and to trust in God. I never thought it would be possible to be comfortable with myself without drugs or alcohol.

I will have three years sober on August 6th, 2019.

"Courage isn't having the strength to go on - it is going on when you don't have the strength." Napoleon Bonaparte

A DARK PATH

By Malachy C.

Growing up I was the class clown. I had parents who loved me unconditionally, classmates who thought I was the funniest, and teachers who could see right through the act. Things took a turn for the worse when my parents got divorced just before middle school.

My first memories of drinking were during family functions. I'm from a large Irish Catholic family and alcohol was the guest of honor at every family function. I started drinking in 7th grade, and by 8th grade I had moved on to marijuana and mind-changing chemicals. My parents recognized my habits at an early age and did the best they could with what they knew. But my behavior was largely out of their control, and by freshman year in high school, I was smoking weed daily, sneaking out of my parents' house, and getting in trouble at school. Drug culture had become my new identity.

My parents sent me to military school at the age of 16. It was around this time that my mom started blogging about my behavior. I felt completely betrayed when I found out that she had made my life public. My self-esteem plummeted, and I felt like everyone around me knew that I wasn't a good person. I started my own personal journal and wrote about how my parents thought they knew everything, but really I was getting away with way more than they were aware of.

The summer I returned home from military school, I went back to my old habits. I needed to be high to feel okay. It was my answer and solution to all of my problems and my personal reward for all of my accomplishments. One night I got drunk, and instead of going home, I drunkenly stumbled into my grandparents' house, and I woke up to my grandfather cleaning my puke from his rug. When my dad picked me up, he took me straight to the police station for a breath test. I was still drunk. He then took me to church and after drove me to a jail about 30 miles away. The two of us sat in the car and stared at the jail for a long time. I asked my dad why we were sitting in front of the jail; he wouldn't answer me so I got out of his truck and started walking. He drove past me and gave me an ultimatum: 'either get in the car and live by our rules (military school) or do your own thing' (freedom).

I chose the latter. He left me on the side of the road, and I thought it was the best thing that had ever happened to me. I called a friend and lived with him for three weeks until my mom found out and took me back in.

Junior year I attended a local public high school, my usage was constant. Shortly after my Senior year, I got a DUI, and both of my parents gave up on me. That's when I started bouncing from friends' houses to local parks to sleep. I kept a blanket and pillow in a tree for sleeping. Somehow my dad got wind of my living situation and asked me to move back in with him and my stepmom. He gave me a job and a room, but, of course, that didn't last long. It was around this time that I had my first girlfriend. My drug usage had gone from bad to out-of-control. My girlfriend realized that she couldn't help me and told me that I was going down a dark path and that she wasn't going to follow me into the darkness.

I tried to get myself together by going to AA meetings. I'd sit in meetings to listen, just waiting to leave and get drunk - my reward for showing up. My lifestyle took a toll on my body, and through a series of unfortunate life choices, I ended up in the hospital with pneumonia, 25 pounds thinner. I was there almost two weeks. On the 12th day, I woke up and realized it was my 21st birthday, there was no way I was going to sit in the hospital on my 21st birthday and waste a chance to party. I started pulling out my IV and told the nurses I was leaving. They asked me to take one last dose of medicine before I left. I woke up the next day; the nurses had given me medicine to put me to sleep and, in reality, they probably ended up saving my life.

I rewarded myself for not drinking by using other drugs. Since alcohol was the problem, in my head, I convinced myself that other drugs were perfectly alright. On my nine-month anniversary of not using alcohol, I went out and got drunk. It was the time of my life, so I decided I could handle alcohol again but in moderation. This plan didn't last a week before I was back to my old ways of drinking.

One night I was sitting in my RV getting drunk and high alone and realized my usage got to a point where when I was sober I needed to be high, and once I was high, I just wanted to be sober.

Some time later, I had my old job back mowing lawns. I got up one day and it was raining so hard that we couldn't work, so I got high. I was lonely and sad and remembered there was something at those AA meetings that I kind of liked. I decided to swing by one. It was at that meeting that I ran into an old high school friend. I didn't even recognize him, but he recognized me. During the meeting I was itching to get high and tried to convince my friend to go party with me, because that's what I always did after AA meetings. Of course, he refused and invited me to lunch instead. From there, he took me to a party and introduced me to his friends in a sobriety group. The party was fun, but I just didn't think it was for me and told them I was going to leave and find some other friends. But they wouldn't let me. They told me they wanted me to stay. They told me they loved hanging out with me and loved me for me.

I was a little suspicious at first, but they just didn't give up on me. I ended up staying with them for two weeks straight and eventually joined their recovery group. In the early days, I got daily phone calls from my new friends. They checked up on me. They made me feel okay. They showed me I was worth it. Now I'm part of the sobriety group and check up on them as well. We all support each other in our recovery and have a ton of fun together.

Getting sober was the best decision I've made in my entire life - hands down. Since getting sober I have an amazing relationship with my family, because I have nothing left to hide. The fellowship and friendships I've made in sobriety are unmatched in comparison to the old crowd of drinking buddies I used to run around with. (In reality, we would all use each other to feel okay about our drinking habits and for other selfish reasons.) Today, I am completely sober and free and happier than I have ever been in my life. I truly feel like a little kid. I own a business and employ young adults who are also in sobriety.

Never give up on yourself; keep your head up; and don't be afraid to ask for help. The highs will be higher. The lows will be lower. If you think your heart can take it, come fly with us.

My past is riddled with chaos, instability, self-centeredness, and pain. I am a broken human, thankfully broken down enough to the point of reaching out for help. We all have shortcomings. Drugs and alcohol made my life unmanageable, and the drugs and the alcohol weren't the problem; they were my solution, and I was the problem. Without drugs and alcohol, I didn't know what to do with my time or how to live happily. Thanks to amazing friends who push me in the right direction and the twelve steps of Alcoholics Anonymous, today I am able to live a fulfilling life with absolutely no drugs or alcohol.

"Life gets better and better as the obsession fades away into the past, right where it belongs." Malachy

INTERNAL ANNIHILATION

By Ari

I was born on December 11th, 2001, in Kansas City, Missouri. During my early childhood, I was a fun and adventurous kid. I can remember the hot Kansas summers, full of the hum of cicadas, waterslides, fireflies, and lemonade stands. I have always been very fortunate to be brought up in a good family with my two loving parents and younger sister, and, as a kid, things were simple and I was happy.

At a very young age I began attending a private school. It wasn't until elementary school that I began getting into mischief. I can't exactly remember what went down, but I can recall many days where I ate lunch in the principal's office. Besides that, I was a very fun and creative kid. I played sports, loved to draw and sing, had friends. Things were simple, and I was happy.

In the fourth grade my family decided to move overseas to Florence, Italy. I had never had to experience being uprooted from the life I had become accustomed to. Suddenly I was dropped into an entirely new way of life. Making friends was never a challenge, however it was a struggle to say goodbye to the friends I had since early childhood. At this time I began seeing a therapist weekly because I began to develop trichotillomania (hair pulling), and I needed a person to talk with about my issues of living away from home. My mom reminds me that the first time I began having meltdowns of not being smart enough or not being good enough began occurring at this time in my life. I can remember one day at school when my teacher was showing us the difference of what good work looked like versus bad work, and when she showed an example of bad work, she held up some of my schoolwork. I can remember the humiliation and shame that brought me in front of all of my peers

Since I was little, I have traveled all over the world and have experienced other places, but living in a different culture gave me a completely new outlook on the world. Luckily, I was still young, and I would be returning to the States the following year to reunite with my life back home. But things were still pretty simple, and I was happy.

Living back in my hometown through the rest of grade school was just as normal as you would expect. I became involved with all of my old activities, friends, and habits. However there now seemed to be a very slight sense of catching up that I had not experienced before, because I had missed out on a year of my life in the States that did not freeze itself for me. There were a few new kids at school who my old friends had known for a while, and I was just beginning to get to know them. Kids began to play new sports that I had never heard of. By the time I started they were already much more experienced than I. However, we were all still young and none of it really ever mattered. Things still remained pretty simple, and I was happy.

By the summer going into 6th grade, one of my friends told me about how his older brother had smoked something called weed. Naturally, I became curious about weed, because his older brother was cool - so weed had to be something that was cool, right? One day while I was playing in a creek down the street from my house, I found a big sealed jar full of weed, rolling papers, grinders, and other things that, at the time, I didn't have any idea what any of it really was; all I knew was that I had found something I wasn't supposed to find, and it was exciting. After doing some research and watching some rolling tutorials on YouTube, I grabbed the jar and took it back to my backyard behind our trampoline and proceeded to roll the worst joint on the face of the planet Earth. I didn't get high, but the feeling of doing something I wasn't supposed to be doing was exhilarating, and that feeling alone was definitely one I wanted to recreate in the future. Things were changing, and I was excited.

Soon after smoking weed for the first time, I began bragging to my friends about how I smoked weed and how I got so high (even though I didn't get high). As expected, everyone thought I was super cool, and I felt like the coolest of my friends. This was just another reason smoking weed was becoming so awesome. It wasn't until I was at my friend's house one day that I smoked weed and actually got high for the first time. I remember that day when I was high; not only did I physically feel amazing, the food was better and everything was funnier, but also all the stress of trying to fit in, of being smart or not, the fear of being judged, and overall stress of life all went away, and I could just have fun like when I was a little kid. I felt comfortable in my own skin and subconsciously knew that this was a feeling that I would want to feel for the rest of my life. Things were changing, and I was excited.

For the rest of that summer I would occasionally smoke weed and, soon after, many of my habits began to change. I started spending my money on weed for the first time rather than food or toys. I began to make new additions to my social circle, many of whom were also getting a head start on acting 21. With these new friends, I became exposed to the less sheltered life of my peers. It was at this time that I experienced my first parties and getting drunk. I was also learning the power that dishonesty had over my parents; if they never knew what I was actually up to, how could I ever get in trouble? However, we were still all innocent kids and never really got into any big trouble. But things were changing, and I was excited.

This routine began to slow down once my 7th grade year of middle school began. Drugs had not yet become a big part of my life and I went back to spending time involved in my sports, friends, and academics as usual. However, by the time I was entering 8th grade, I was smoking weed on an almost regular basis. I had also surrounded myself with people who also liked to do drugs like me. Things were fun and seemed innocent, and there was always that thrill of doing what I knew I wasn't supposed to be doing. Eventually, I started getting caught, which inevitably led to losing trust with my parents. But at this point my parents were not very concerned, so I was never in any serious trouble. I was also beginning to slowly get a reputation around school of being a "bad kid", and I remember the feeling of isolation that that brought.

My first year in high school is where things really took a turn for the worse. I had become comfortable and used to the way middle school was; however, when I started high school, I was one of the youngest at the school, and it was very intimidating. Leading up to my freshman year I'd known about other drugs and never thought I would actually try them, but they were always intriguing. I became friends with a kid in the grade above me, and he told me about how he did, and had access to, LSD. I was hooked on the thought of taking a crazy drug like this. The first time I tried LSD it was like that first time I smoked weed, where all of my problems melted away. The same feeling of wanting to start doing this more often came up. From there, I began smoking weed more heavily and doing LSD almost every weekend. The more and more I used, the more and more I felt distanced from my peers and felt isolated.

By now word had spread that I was a "druggie" and many of my friends' parents began not wanting me over at their houses. My parents became more and more aware of the trouble I was getting myself into and decided to have me start seeing a therapist, as well as drug testing me weekly. They didn't allow me to have money and put many other restrictions on me. I was on a very short leash, however, as I'm sure you all know, if there's a will there's a way. And I always found a way. This is when I started sneaking out, stealing my parents' car, and risking getting in trouble with the law just to get my fix or to have one night of fun with my friends.

Eventually I began getting more curious about new drugs. This is when I was introduced to drugs like whippets, codeine, and Xanax. With Xanax it was really easy for me to stop caring about all of the stressful and uncomfortable aspects about my life, whether it was that I didn't feel smart enough, wasn't good enough at this or that, or so and so did not like me - and the list goes on. The uncomfortable feeling of being alone in the world began to creep further and further into my mind, and my anxiety and stress became a daily dilemma. But my ego was always too big to admit to myself that I could have these problems. The way I coped with these feelings was by taking on a role which wasn't really me. I remember one night while I was hallucinating on LSD, I stood in front of my bathroom mirror and told myself, "Ari, this is the person you should be. People will like you if you act like this." I gave so much power to what everyone thought about me that it made me insane. I can also remember vivid moments after waking up from a night of using, feeling drowsy from the night before and thinking just how miserable I was to be living in this vicious cycle of needing to smoke or drop and pop something. In these desperate moments of clarity, I remember telling myself that I wish I could quit or that I want to change something, only to find myself back to my regularly scheduled routine of using not even 20 minutes later.

It is extremely moving now looking back at my life through a sober lens, because all of my emotions and feelings at that time were almost completely masked by my use. I didn't want to feel because not feeling was better than feeling anything at all, and when I did have these moments of clarity, my ego was too big and delusional to admit things were bad. However, looking back on my life, I am finally allowing myself to feel and understand what I truly felt in the low moments of my life.

As my freshman year of high school came to a close, I was already a complete train wreck. Most parents were hesitant to have me over, trust between my parents and me did not exist, almost all freedoms were lost, and I was internally miserable to my core. This would all begin to change after a single night. The Thursday night of March 30th, 2017, a couple of my friends had decided to sneak out with their parents' car and pick me up. What we weren't expecting that night was to get shot at, leaving a bullet hole in the car, and then getting pulled over later that night with that bullet hole still in the car. My parents were done with me, and I came face to face with an ultimatum: either go to military school or check into a recovery program. I brushed off their concerns for me, assuming they were bluffing, and carried on as if nothing had happened the prior night. However, that Friday after school they picked me up and drove me straight to a young people's recovery program (The Crossroads Program), and that is where I have spent the last two and a half years of my life.

I can't quite remember a lot from my first couple of months in recovery or even why I wanted to stay. I think I began to stick around because since that first day checking out the program I was immediately surrounded by people who showered me with love - with no expectation of it being reciprocated. I couldn't quite understand why they wanted to be my friend so badly, but I didn't really care. I just knew that I felt accepted by these people. The longer I stayed, the faster I began to fall in love with the idea of recovery - where everyone was working together to improve each other's lives and people genuinely cared for each other's wellbeing. While I was using, I viewed most of my friendships as transactions: I'm your friend because you give me this, and you are mine because I gave you that. In recovery, I found that the love I received from my friends was an unconditional love that I had never really been exposed to. They didn't care if I tried to push them away or tried to be someone who I wasn't. They just viewed me as another sick addict who needed as much love as I could get.

Time went on and things started to become clearer in my life once I declared defeat to my drug use. The thinking that got me into recovery was that no one comes to recovery on a winning streak by any means, and, if my own thinking and decisions led me here, I probably didn't think too logically. I was soon beginning to find a purpose in my recovery; I had obtained 30 days of consistent sobriety in my outpatient program and was beginning to get honest and to open up about the craziness I had trapped in the depths of my head for so many years. Don't get me wrong, things were definitely not perfect, but as long as I was striving to progress myself in my day to day life, that's all that mattered, and I knew that I didn't have to work on these issues of recovery by myself.

Around my first month in recovery an old friend of mine committed suicide. I saw my friends around me become very emotional about this tragedy, but for some reason my years of numbing had not allowed me to feel very much emotion. I remember nights of trying to force myself to cry or feel sad or anything at all, but the truth was I was unable to feel yet. However, eventually I began to experience my emotions for the first time in a long time, and these feelings were strange and uncomfortable, but at least I felt something. The challenge here was to accept the feelings I had tried avoiding for so many years and face my problems head on. This is when I began to experience real growth.

By the time that I'm writing this, I will have a little over two and a half years sober. I've experienced pain but also the happiness and freedom that lies on the other side of that pain. I've allowed myself to go from an empty shell of a human being who was so numbed by drugs that he could not physically express emotion, to a man who has cried tears of joy out of genuine happiness and gratitude for his life. The life that my recovery has given me was that missing puzzle piece that I was always looking for to feel okay. I'd just been looking for it in all the wrong places. I am now in a position to reach out to newcomers in recovery and give the love and experience that was so openly and freely given to me when I was new, which is possibly one of the coolest opportunities I have in my life today.

"There is comfort in knowing that you aren't alone, that what you're feeling isn't unusual, and that there is a solution."
Anonymous

BY THE GRACE OF GOD

By Anonymous

For the first time in a long time, I'm lost for words. I'm sitting here trying to think about how I can describe my life leading up to and in recovery. I guess the best place to start is going into high school. I was an extremely lost kid who had no idea what he wanted to do with his life and far less of an idea of who I even wanted to be on any given day. I had spent the previous three to four years relatively alone because I was way too anxious to be in public, and I also didn't have the best experience when it came to having friends. I was also pretty sad. I don't want to use the word depressed because I feel like that word is grossly overused, so that being said, I spent a lot of nights wondering if life was worth it and if I wanted to continue living.

Fast forward to sophomore year. I was introduced to the thing that changed everything: weed. The first time I smoked weed was with my friend who introduced me to a kid who was known to smoke at our school, and they invited me to come hangout with them. As soon as I took the first hit, it felt like every problem I had in my life had been instantly answered. I was no longer sad; I was no longer anxious; and, most importantly, I was finally okay in my own skin. I could hold conversations with people, and I could be the "me" I always wanted to be.

This is where everything changed. I started off a fairly innocent kid - definitely not a rule breaker - but once I smoked weed for the first time, I spiraled quickly. It became the only thing I looked forward to. I would smoke every day after school and even sometimes before I went to school, and all my money was going right to my habit. After about a month, I decided it was best to take a break, and I spent my summer going into my junior year saving money trying to be a good kid because I didn't want to see my life go up in flames. As soon as junior year started though, I was right back in it. I had found a girl, and I was in love and wanted to impress and win her over at all costs, and that involved smoking again. So I started and this time it didn't stop there. Within a month of smoking again and getting this feeling that I loved so much, I wanted more, so I started trying more drugs, firstly starting to drink and then trying things like Xanax and others just trying to feel okay. This led to me being 16 years old waiting for my next high and eventually taking whatever anyone handed me because I could not bear to live without being high. Around this time I discovered I could abuse my Adderall, so that became a huge part of my life, taking it around the clock and making sure I would never come down.

Fast-forward another two months to November. I tried cocaine for the first time and instantly fell in love. I immediately quit my job and spent every penny I had on as much as I could get. Within a week, I had resorted to selling drugs in order to get more and couldn't sleep or even eat without it. With the newfound confidence I had found in coke, I ended up confessing my love to the girl I previously mentioned and got turned down. Everything hit me like a brick. I didn't like my life. I didn't like getting high. I had to get high to be okay. This is when I decided that I wanted to end it all, and the first attempt on my life happened that night when I tried to overdose on cocaine mixed with alcohol.

Obviously, that didn't end up working out, and I was devastated. That is when I realized that I had a problem. I tried to hide it as much as I could, but I only made it two weeks before I was arrested for paraphernalia and had to face the fact that I was an addict. I was immediately sent to a support group type rehab where I continued to drink because I was just an addict; I didn't have a problem with alcohol, or at least I didn't think I did.

After one month of trying to drink my way through recovery, I ended up getting alcohol poisoning and passing out in my car with all of my windows down on a 15 degree night, completely covered in puke. I was found a couple of hours later by my parents, due to them tracking me, and instantly their worst nightmare appeared true - I was presumed dead. Luckily, they got me into somewhere warm and were able to clean me up enough for me to come back into consciousness, and that is when I realized that this was no longer about me. I was ruining my family, leaving them in constant fear that when I walked out of the door that morning it be the last time they'd ever see me. I have been sober ever since that night. My official sobriety date is January 23rd 2016. When first getting sober, someone told me getting sober is the easy part; staying sober is the hard part, and boy were they right. Getting off of drugs and alcohol was easy. I just had to stay away from any place that any drugs and alcohol would be available.

Then the hard part started: admitting that I was in the wrong and that I was the problem. I don't have a weed problem or a coke or an alcohol problem. I have a "me" problem.

When I first joined the program of Alcoholics Anonymous, I was put off by the 12 steps that were put in front of me, but after about 6 months of trying to live my life my own way and failing miserably to be happy, I decided to give the 12 steps a chance. The 12 steps have changed my life in a way that I could've never imagined. I never thought I would find happiness without being under the influence and never thought I would be able to be in social situations completely sober and still be able to function. But here we are, just days after I celebrated three and a half years sober, and I have a life I could never have imagined. I am extremely grateful for the recovery that I have found in these last couple of years and even more grateful for the people I have met along the way. Even though it has never been easy and life happened and knocked me down, I am still able to sit here today and say that I am happy, joyous, and free.

"I'm not telling you this is going to be easy. I'm telling you it's going to be worth it."
Anonymous

I'LL BE HAPPY WHEN...

By Charlie

In my early childhood, I was well behaved and active, but I was always confused with myself. At times I would fit in socially, and then, so quickly into the next year, my life felt like it was falling apart over and over. This happened all throughout elementary school, and when things would start to fall apart, it got bad quickly. When I felt bullied, it felt like the end of the world. I started to feel depressed when I was in the 5th grade, and it was at this time that I was also diagnosed with Tourette's syndrome. Even though my tics have drastically reduced over the years, they still occur when I am stressed, and I still get insecure.

Eventually, I learned to use the things I was good at in order to try to make more friends, such as athletics, being mean to other kids, and acting like an idiot to make other kids laugh. This would work for a while, but there were always people (other kids) that would eventually get into my head and make me feel like nothing. I was always pretty good with keeping my feelings to myself, and no one knew what was going on in my brain.

When middle school came around, and before I had ever done drugs, the feelings of worthlessness grew. I felt like no one really liked me, and I was just a burden in a world that didn't matter to me. But once more, I just kept putting on this alternative persona of a kid who loves his life and is friends with everyone. Transitioning to middle school was hard for me. I was comfortable hanging out with the same people and doing the same things all of the time, but this was not the case once I arrived in middle school. I lost a lot of close friends as they went off to hang out with other kids, but I also made new "friends". These new people who I started hanging around changed my personality; they weren't the best influence on me. I picked up bad habits like stealing, bullying, doing poorly in school, and behaving like the kids who made me feel like nothing. After a while, I realized how my behavior and actions were impacting my life, but my desire for popularity and being accepted became more important to me.

I started to try harder to fit in, and soon enough, I had an abundance of "friends" and popularity. I had all of the things that I thought would make me happy, and yet, things kept getting worse. By the end of middle school, I had developed a really bad eating disorder. I'd skip meals, workout, and become overly focused on my appearance. And I became so depressed; I felt insane. Freaking out on my family was a regular occurrence at home. I wanted an escape from life and didn't know what to do. No psychologist or psychiatrist was able to help me and I was just stuck.

Toward the end of 8th grade, I was introduced to alcohol. At this point in my life, I had managed to steal a beer or two from my dad, a sip of wine from my mom, or a shot from my sister...but this was different. Some friends and I snuck into a liquor cabinet and stole handles of gin, whiskey, and vodka. I don't remember much, but I do remember that we had no idea what we were doing and that I felt like I was temporarily released from this feeling of being stuck, and my worries disappeared. That night I kept drinking until I passed out and woke up the next day having those same feelings of depression and nothingness.

Soon after middle school ended, all my friends started to occasionally smoke weed, and I was scared for a bit because of the things my mom told me it does to you. One day I was home alone, and my friends asked if they could come over and smoke in my backyard. The next thing I know, I'm watching my friends light up using a Gatorade bottle with tin foil as a homemade pipe. I see them laughing and having fun. I didn't understand why they were able to have so much fun, and I was still blank on the inside. They told me to try it, but I told them no. They asked again and again, and eventually, I fed into the feeling of not caring what happens next and wanting to fit in, and so I tried it. Everything after that was just that feeling of caring less. I was in a mindset of being introduced to a whole new world, one that seemed like happiness to me. That summer, smoking weed started as a weekend thing and drinking was only for parties. This boundary didn't last long, and by the end of the summer I was smoking multiple times a day, even by myself, and drinking whenever I could get my hands on alcohol. I didn't know too many people who shared this love and lifestyle of getting wasted all the time, but the people who I did know that were willing to share my new hobby became my new friends.

Freshman year started and school was on the bottom of my priority list. Every day was the same: "How can I get high today?" I was so excited for high school. I'd heard the stories of parties, girls, and this was becoming a normal thing for me too. After a few weeks, I discovered so many more people like me, through football, classes, and even social media. I was making "friends" all the time. I would spend time jumping around friend groups and getting worse and worse grades, but nothing mattered because I could erase it all with the use of alcohol and drugs. Freshman year was going well, or so I thought, until my parents started catching me high all the time, and we slowly grew apart. Then the people who I thought were friends just liked to use me, and smoking was getting more and more dull, and alcohol was getting expensive.

January of my freshman year was the first time I gave into the constant depression inside me and attempted suicide. My parents were concerned and sent me to an adolescent psychiatric hospital where I felt imprisoned for the next week. When I got out, everything just got worse, I fought with my parents constantly and would avoid them as much as possible. I was angry and felt like I needed more and more drugs to survive each day. My very few friends that were actually good for me abandoned me because they thought I was going crazy. At this point in my life, I only ever thought about some way to get myself high. I started drinking more by myself and smoking every chance I got.

Eventually my parents couldn't take any more of my freak-outs and crazed fighting with them, and I forced them to kick me out. By now child family services was working with our family, and I was staying at homes and with people who weren't stable for me. I would leave home or get kicked out a few times over the next year or so, and I couch hopped or even spend the night in a field if I had nowhere else to go. By the time April came around, I was not the kid that everyone knew who was nice and polite and had good things going for him. I was failing school, robbing people, affiliating with bad people, and felt nothing for my family. I would tell myself I wouldn't make it past the age of 18. One morning I was fighting with my dad and overdosed on some pills right in front of him. This became a recurring event - me going back to Marillac (the psych hospital), getting released, and throwing more of what I thought was my worthless life away. I kept going on.

My life continued in chaos, and in May, my dad found me on the floor of my basement after I had tried to hang myself. Luckily, my weight broke the ceiling. I could see the terrified look in his eyes and knew he was scared. He was scared of me and scared that one of these times I would succeed in taking my life or doing something irreversible. My parents tried so many therapists, medications, and even tried to send me away to in-patient treatment programs all over the country, but I was unwilling to try anything. I threatened to run away or get kicked out of military school if they tried to send me away.

By summertime before my sophomore year, I was just hanging around people who were just as addicted to this feeling as I was. At this point, drugs were a necessity and wouldn't stop me from hating the way I looked, the way I felt, and the feeling of a meaningless life. My life and my perspective on everything was so warped; I thought that there was no point to anything and people were just to be exploited to get things that I wanted.

On June 29, I was home because I was grounded and the only thing I could feel that day was loneliness. I decided in the morning that later that afternoon, when my parents left, I would do everything in my power to end my life of misery. I don't remember much, but I remember drinking a lot of vodka (that I kicked down a locked door to get) and taking pills and finally using a kitchen knife to cut my stomach. I was taken to a hospital, and they sent me to Children's Mercy Hospital downtown. My heart rate was so low, and they could not figure out why, until they realized that it was from all the years of not eating. My heart was starting to fail. I was transferred out south to the Children's Mercy eating disorder floor where I was watched 24 hours a day and put on a re-feeding program. I did nothing but lie in bed all day. The only thing that was going through my mind that entire time was, "When can I get out of here?" I didn't get to have many visitors except my family and a very few select friends. Because I was on the re-feeding floor, I could not exercise, much less leave the room, and so I didn't have much to do. All I felt was that I was going crazy. After a month they tried to find a place to take me, but all of the drug treatment facilities refused me because of my heart rate and eating disorder diagnosis. And the eating disorder clinics often did not treat drug use, so the hospital sent me back to Marillac for a week.

When I was finally released from Marillac after an entire month of hospitalization and little socialization, I was taken immediately to the Ozarks with my family for a family vacation. I just wanted to go home. I immediately got into a fight with my parents and took off walking. Eventually I hitchhiked a ride for a few miles, and my dad came to get me then took me home. The plan was for me to stay sober after already having around 40 days sober, but I did the only thing I knew how to do. Right when my dad fell asleep, I snuck out and got high.

Two days later, child family services drug tested me, and I failed. The disappointment I felt from family was typical, so I didn't think anything of it. Life was becoming more chaotic and unmanageable after the hospital, and I developed bulimia and realized I needed help but didn't know how or what to do.

Sophomore year began and I would skip around 3 days a week to go get high and started to use LSD. I started dabbling around with other drugs like cocaine, Xanax, and codeine. School was a social environment for me, and I had no interest in education or a future for myself. Eventually, the school filed for truancy and luckily nothing else. I had to show up for court and the judge threatened to take my phone and laptop and ordered a follow up drug test in a month.

The following November, my sister told me she was going to try getting sober from alcohol and asked me to come with her to a meeting. I told her I would give it a shot, but most of my motivation was that I had 60 days to get clean for the drug test. When I first showed up to a meeting it just felt unnatural - there were all these kids who had so much love and joy that it seemed like a joke. But when I met with the counselors and people in this sobriety group, I felt like they actually understood what I was going through, and they did. The feeling of being able to relate to a number of people helped me feel like I actually fit in.

The beginning of sobriety was hard for me. Learning to trust people and be willing to work through my past and daily problems was not what I had in mind when I considered getting sober. Most of my life, I changed how I acted and looked just to fit in with certain people. I was finally learning to be myself, and not having the stress or anxiety, the need for drugs and alcohol, or the constant fighting with my parents was such a freeing feeling. Initially, after I passed my drug test, I was planning on going back to my previous life. But that changed when I took a look at myself and realized that I was truly happy for once. I began to see that all of the great things I had, like true friends, great family relationships, a car, and life goals were worth more than chasing that high.

In sobriety, I have learned how to handle my own pathology and how to deal with problems with the help of God and my friends. Recovery has brought me so many memorable times: when I was newly sober I went on a road trip to Arkansas; for the New Year's celebration the sobriety group had a love meeting where we could express how much we mean to each other and share the feeling of love around; and about two weeks ago I went on a camping trip and met so many new people I wanted to share and receive love with. Now, as a sober 16-year-old, I can keep a steady job, live at home, get to see my older sister get sober with me, do well in school, and live my life everyday happy. I also have true friendships, learned coping skills, and have the love of the group to rely on. I have goals and dreams and am working a solid 12-step program. I have become a leader and learned how to set an example for others by continuing to work hard and showing up for people in my group. I have invested the last 245 days to being sober and don't regret any of it.

"Success is the sum of small efforts repeated day in and day out." Robert Collier

JUST ONE FRIEND

By R. S.

I've moved a lot throughout my life, and the amount of times my family has moved has been detrimental to my health. After not staying in the same place for longer than four years, my family ended up moving to Las Vegas. The environment I was raised in in Vegas was very party and drug related. Having a party every weekend was part of my routine; it became a ritual. Every party would be a game to me - how can I show everyone that I am "cool". The goal was to drink the most and party harder than anyone. I usually ended up waking up and not remembering anything about the previous night.

After my parents realized that our Vegas life wasn't working out the best for my siblings and me, we decided to move to Kansas. At this time, they did not know about my drug abuse. Moving to Kansas was a big blur to me, and this was around the 25th time moving houses for me. I didn't know where I was or where I was going. My parents eventually enrolled me in a very small, private high school that I found no interest in attending. Coming from a background of partying and having fun, I was integrated into a place where maybe only two kids smoked weed on weekends. This was new. I asked myself how could they do that? I could barely be satisfied with two drinks or a few blunts. Having that realization, I made the decision to drink, smoke, and consume drugs alone practically every day.

Drinking alcohol alone started at a young age for me. It felt warm; it felt like the best thing in the world. Being in new social environments every few years made it difficult for me to assimilate to reality, and so I drank. Nothing beat the feeling of being drunk or high for me, so that's how I lived. Reaching a point of dissatisfaction, I would try to reach out of my social situation and make friends. I tried and I tried, but I never let anyone be my friend. On the other hand, I met a guy who is one of my best friends today. Drew (not his real name) told me that he didn't party or drink. He told me, "We can only hang out when you are sober." At that point, I disregarded his comments and moved on.

Soon after, we had a school trip overseas, but I did not want to go because I did not like anyone. That didn't matter because my parents forced me to attend. Before the trip I had my last joint I've ever had to this day. On the trip, Drew, the guy who wouldn't hangout with me unless I was sober, reached out to me. Turns out, in this controlled environment, I couldn't drink or do drugs, so I was the perfect target for his help. He had been sober for almost a year. Drew and I would talk over and over about life and how we don't have to drink or smoke to be happy. Those conversations saved my life. I made a conscious decision that I needed to stop abusing or I'd end up six feet under. We traveled around the hotels and smoked cigarettes on hotel roofs. This was fun; this was the life.

Sooner or later the trip was over, and Drew, still my only friend, asked me to come to an AA meeting with him. I denied him for a few weeks in a row. I thought I could do it all myself. After having the constant feeling of emptiness every day, I started to get depressed. I did not want to live; I could not live without drugs or alcohol. My need to fill this empty void led me to constant physical activity and non-stop basketball. This did not help me at all though. It just dug a deeper hole of emptiness and depression.

After an awakening, I decided to go to a younger people's AA meeting with my friend. Being there for a short time made me realize that I do not have to be drunk or high to be happy. I decided to go for a month or two, until I signed up for their outpatient program. Every day for four hours during the afternoon, I would help solve my problems with my fellow young alcoholics in recovery. At times it has been stressful and confusing, and at times it's been fun and easy. Getting sober was a really fast roller coaster, but, at the end, the roller coaster stops... until you ride another one. I learned a lot about myself. I learned that I am a fear hole. I would be scared of everything, from girls to stepping off a two feet ledge. The biggest new habit that I have learned is walking through fear. After walking through fear every day, I knew not to take myself so seriously. I became comfortable in my skin and was able to actually communicate with people and enjoy life. Sobriety has given me and will give me something to live for, a purpose that I have searched for my whole life. Being "other centered" every day gives me the will to strive for a better self and a better world.

At first, it was hard for me to grasp that during meetings I am in a room with 50 people, and I can name them all and call them my friends. Getting high, I only remembered what people looked like, how many drugs they had, or if they were "cool". It's been a spiritual awakening for me, and I realize that I never want to ruin this.

Sobriety has made my life substantially better. Now I go to school and want to work and learn. I talk to people every day and enjoy being interpersonal. With the skills sobriety has given me, I am able to function as an adult and be responsible. I am positive that I am going to be successful and be a positive influence for everyone around me for the rest of my life.

"Not feeling is no replacement for reality. Your problems today are still your problems tomorrow." Larry Michael Dredla

VISIONS & VOICES

By George

I had great parents and a good home. When I look back, I didn't have any problems as a young kid, just an underlying feeling of not fitting in.

In 2005, I moved to Kansas City. I was in the middle of second grade and started at a local Christian school. Making friends was always difficult, and by third grade, I was the target of my classmates' bullying. I was constantly made fun of and never felt like I was a part of things. I wasn't good at sports and preferred science and learning. Plus, I was always a smart ass, and I guess that got on people's nerves. A few times my mom called the school to complain about kids bullying me, and the principal would have the kids apologize to me in person. That, of course, didn't make a difference and probably made it worse. Needless to say I didn't have a lot of friends. In spite of all of my lack of friends, I was a GOOD KID! I didn't fight with my parents; I went to church every Sunday; I did pretty much everything right.

Things started to take a turn for the worse when we moved to a new neighborhood at the start of sixth grade. When seventh grade rolled around, I was fed up with being made fun of and not having any friends. There were only 28 kids in my class, so it was pretty difficult to break into new groups. At the same time, I was in Boy Scouts. I remember going through puberty kind of early and feeling pretty desperate. I didn't have a girlfriend and girls really didn't show any interest in me at all. Out of desperation and loneliness, I had a homosexual experience with a boy in my Scout group. I never talked about it - I totally repressed the experience and memory.

Now truly tired of not having friends and getting made fun of, I found a new group of kids in my new neighborhood. We started hanging out, but I still never felt like I fit in - I just couldn't shake the feeling of not being good enough. Eventually I made friends with one kid in my neighborhood known to be "the bad kid". My new friend knew of an older brother who smoked weed, and at first, I just thought I'd wait to do that in high school. Instead, that summer (the summer before eighth grade), I smoked weed for the first time. I smoked one or two joints and have a vivid memory of the feeling of finally being ok. I thought, "This is the answer. This is going to make things right. I've found the answer to all my problems." Since I was so young, it was tough to get weed, but whenever I had the opportunity, I would smoke.

That same year, I got my first girlfriend. We had an "interesting" relationship, to say the least. We ended up staying together for two years, but she had a lot of anxiety and depression. We were completely codependent. She never wanted me to smoke weed, so I hid it. Having a girlfriend didn't necessarily help me with my friends. They made fun of me for dating her, so I often tried to get distance from her. It was tough though, because she texted me constantly about how she wanted to die, and I'd end up staying up until 3 or 4 in the morning trying to help her. This became a running theme for me: I would help people solve their problems and feel completely responsible for them.

By freshman year, my stress over this girl and my friends was really ramping up. It became a year of firsts. I ate mushrooms in school for the first time. It still baffles me that I made it through that school day. I started drinking a lot more. I tried cocaine for the first time that year as well. I kept trying to distance myself from my girlfriend, but she tried to commit suicide, and so the cycle continued. While she was in the psych ward for depression, I finally felt like I had time to relax and do my own thing for a bit. She eventually got a little better, and we started a cycle of partying, having sex, and going our separate ways. It was a weird relationship of codependency and loneliness. It's really sad to look back on now.

Around this time, I tried acid for first time - or what I thought was acid. I ended up taking a risky research chemical instead. The experience was intense and scary. I don't remember a lot, but I apparently stripped all my clothes off for one hour and yelled at my parents and rocked back and forth. But, like always, I lied to get myself out of the situation and tried to regain their trust.

Eventually, my relationship with this girl ended completely, and I felt a weight was finally off my shoulders. Now I started drinking daily, doing acid, and eating mushrooms. I did try painkillers, and luckily I didn't like it. In spite of this, I still didn't fit in in high school - it was just a new school with the same old themes. In my school, the go-to word if you weren't liked was to call you a "fag". No one knew about my early experience and how being called a fag affected my mental state. My coping mechanism was to tell myself that I didn't care what anyone thinks, but, in reality, I cared very deeply about what people thought. (Almost everything I did is because I wanted people to view me a certain way - in a better light.) So those insults really hurt, and being left out really hurt. I know now that the source of a lot of shame is to tell someone they aren't good enough until they believe it.

Junior year I needed more money to buy weed. I was hanging out with a few shady kids (drop outs), and we had a plan to get money. I took Xanax to get high so I could be "ok" with stealing from people's cars. Deep down this was completely against my upbringing and morals, so I had to get high so I didn't have to think about it. I did this for about a month, and I eventually OD'd on Xanax. I was found in a sketchy area face down and woke up in hospital a day later. Once again, I had to lie my way out of a situation.

Senior year I got kicked out of the private Catholic school I attended. The administration searched my phone and found things about drugs. I lied to my parents and told them I made a mistake but was better now. I always said whatever it took to get what I wanted. Of course, I still got high every day.

The rest of senior year I went to a public school, which was a cakewalk. I skipped class and went to get high a lot. I met a new girl, and we smoked a lot together and skipped class. We shared a dream of going west and starting a commune. She was dealing with anxiety and her parents' divorce, so she started to spend the night at my house. My dad was not ok with it, but I once again manipulated my way into getting what I wanted.

All during senior year I'd hang with my new girlfriend and get high. We went to a rave and I took acid. She'd never done it before, so when I freaked out she couldn't help me. I had to explain to her that it's just what happens with acid - you go down a rabbit hole, and it's not fun. She asked me not to do acid anymore, so I reluctantly agreed to stop. I continued to smoke weed. I tried to help her with her anxiety, but it didn't help. I wanted to be the knight in shining armor, but it doesn't work that way, so it caused lots of turmoil in our relationship. I was frustrated, and I said screw it - I am going out and taking acid. I broke up with her the next morning, but she came to my house and banged on the door. Against the better judgment of everyone, I took her back.

We moved out to Washington together even though I knew it was a bad idea. My plan was to snowboard and grow weed and live in paradise freely. My parents wouldn't help if I wasn't going to school, so I agreed to go for one semester. My girlfriend had zero plans, so we ended up living in the same dorm together. She signed up for all the same classes, and we spent 100% of our time together. It was really dysfunctional. I ended up dropping out because I was carrying the weight of school for both of us. We moved to an apartment and our relationship started to go downhill.

I started growing mushrooms and planned to sell them to make money and live the way I wanted to. The first batch I grew I ate. I had a vision while high which told me that it wasn't my path to sell the mushrooms. (This sounds weird, but it's true.) I really enjoyed the science behind growing mushrooms, so I just grew them, ate them, and gave them away. We used one bedroom for my mushroom growing operation, and the other was our bedroom. Eventually we broke up, and I was finally on my own. Again, I felt a weight was lifted off my shoulders. But that underlying loneliness and low self worth came back. Here I was alone with the mushrooms, and I start to make another chemical - DMT. I was playing mad scientist in my apartment.

I didn't have many friends - I kept pushing them away. Around this same time I started to do fire performances - like a fire dance. I practiced a lot and went to a park and met a guy who was way better, so I learned from him. He was homeless and his friends were too. I had found a captive group of friends in them who were always in one spot. They were a group of people I could run to. I'm not sure it was true friendship, but they had great acid and it was basically free. So I started taking acid again. Eventually, I decided to clean my apartment and took this acid that a guy had given me. It kicked in, and I wondered what I was going to do now; I immediately locked eyes with this book on my counter that a girl had left behind. I read the book, and it spoke about coincidences not being coincidences. I had this transcendental experience and called my mom and apologize to her for all I'd done.

Nothing changes though.

I kept doing acid and hanging with my homeless park friends. I also started to get really paranoid that someone would find me and figure out what I was doing. I grew more and more paranoid. One week I went to a festival in the woods. (It's called the rainbow gathering, and it's not a great place.) I took acid every day. When I came back home, I really started to get full-scale psychosis; I was scared people were out to get me. In fact, an undercover agent did come to the park, and I really started to go out of my mind. So now I was legitimately being followed, and that, coupled with my own paranoia, meant that I believed I could trust no one. I was going insane. Everyone said to stop acid, but I just couldn't stop. Eventually I got so scared that I was going to go to prison that I had no idea what to do with my life. I tossed around going sober, but I still didn't get my shit together. I got so low that I decided to move back home. I had to do something, or I'd kill myself because I just could not go to jail.

That night I went to the desert to eat mushrooms and asked God what to do with my life. I know that sounds so insane, but I ate the shrooms and didn't feel anything. It was very underwhelming and disheartening, so I walked out of the desert the next morning and felt desperate. At some point, I got hit with an overwhelming message: "Don't worry. You are not going to jail." This calmed me down and brought me back to earth. I made a resolve to change and get better and decided to definitely move back home. My mom helped me move home, and in the car I told her a little of what happened and how I was going off the deep end. I told her I was going to become an alcoholic and not do drugs.

For two or three months, I just drank a lot and stayed away from drugs. I just needed anything to feel different. I had been going out to bars every night with a buddy; he paid for my drinks and I'd drive him home. He'd smoke weed in front of me, and I wouldn't. But one night I broke down and smoked. Soon after, I started smoking weed, and eventually doing cocaine. I started doing it all day and night. I was going back down this spiral. I just continued to have this overwhelming loneliness, and I'd text everyone and no one would text back. All I did was get high alone. Eventually I started doing Ketamine again - I'd heard it's supposed to help with depression. I tried to medicate myself. I would sort of pass out for an hour and come back out having gleaned nothing and feeling horrible.

I was at a low point where the very last thing I did to help myself didn't work. It was July 2018, and I was driving to my job. I was so sad and lonely and a song came on the radio talking about needing help. I thought about it for a second and realized I needed help. So I was resolved to get help, but I had no idea who to talk to or how to get help. Two days later, I was coming home from work. I always went to the same gas station to get cigarettes, but this day, for some reason, I went to a different one. What do you know but an old friend I used to get high with was there! I jumped out of my car and jumped into his. We talked and talked, and he told me he'd been sober for a year now. I couldn't comprehend that. My friend and the word sober didn't go together. He asked me about my life, and I told him how horrible it was. He dropped everything he was doing and talked to me that night about his recovery program. I met a friend of his who gave me the card for the program's counselor.

It took me a few days, but I smoked the last of my weed, did the last of my cocaine, and drank the end of my alcohol, and made the call that I wanted to get help. I know none of this would have happened if I hadn't had the vision that I wanted to get sober.

I know that my recovery was a plan from God - divine intervention. I showed up to my first meeting still drunk and high. But that was my last time getting drunk and high. My first day sober was July 24, 2018, and I've never looked back.

"If you seek the perfect high, find it in yourself." Shel Silverstein

FALLING SHORT

By Ben

I am a teen in recovery, and I got and stayed sober when I was 17. Here is my story and the journey it took me to get to where I am today.

First, I need to give a little bit of backstory. Almost all my family members are alcoholics and drug addicts in recovery. When my mother was in her early childhood, her parents were about 19 or 20 when they drove drunk and crashed their car and died. When I was a child, I was diagnosed with severe depression and anxiety. I saw numerous therapists and was prescribed numerous medications, but none of it worked or ever lasted that long. I felt like an outcast - somehow, I was able to feel lonely in a room full of other people. Ultimately, I felt broken. I was able to watch my friends have fun and be happy, and I never quite understood why I could never have that. I desperately wanted to seek other people's approval and was so terrified of what people thought of me. I wanted people to like me so much that it became the most important thing in my life, and, in doing so I thought I had to be the best at whatever I did. When it came to sports or being the most athletic or being the funniest guy in the room, I'd set these expectations on myself, and I fell short almost every time.

Later in elementary school, I started self-harming to cope with my problems of feeling unwanted or feeling like a burden. When I moved to middle school, I began to use drugs and alcohol for the first time. I still vividly remember the first time I got high. The first time I used, I felt like it was something I had been searching for my whole life. I felt like I was on a roller coaster, and I never wanted it to end. My feelings of being unwanted or a burden or my fear of what people thought of me went away in that moment. That had been what I wanted to happen my whole life.

At that moment, I had decided that what I wanted to be the best at was doing more drugs than anyone I knew, and I wanted to try every drug possible.

When high school came around, that was bad news. I went from this seemingly innocent kid to this sketchy crazy kid that people didn't want to be around. I had decided that drugs and using were more important than sports and academics, and by the time I was 16, I found my new love and her name was opiates. Everything changed once I started using opiates. I started to grow a physical addiction to drugs, and then I found I needed to use drugs to function. I needed to start making money to afford drugs, but I couldn't keep a job because most employers don't like it when you show up to work high on pills. So I started to steal to get high. Then it turned into needing to sell drugs so I could afford them. At this point I was starting to lose all my friends. I would make new ones, and then I'd steal from them, so they would stop being my friends. At some point I stole from my only friends, and then they tried jumping and robbing me. Then it was just me, and I convinced myself that I didn't need friends if I had drugs. I mean if you get high by yourself, it just means more drugs and alcohol for you, right? Unfortunately, it wasn't that simple. I felt like I just went through the motions every day. At that point, I believed that I was just a waste of space and that the world would be a better place without me. I felt like a robot and would get high to try to feel anything. My life was falling apart and it only got worse.

I was just 16 when I got my first drug charges. I kept getting in trouble with the law and ended up in my first treatment thanks to the cop car that dropped me off. It was hell. I didn't plan on going to meetings afterwards or bettering myself whatsoever. I just wanted to go home and go back to what I was doing, but I just couldn't understand for the life of me why people I knew could get high and have normal lives. For me, it was like every time I used my life would fall apart. Soon I would get out and live at my grandma's over an hour away from home. I lived there for about two weeks and didn't use. I would just sit in her basement and watch TV and rarely leave the couch. I had fallen into a depression. I was all alone and believed that I was the only person I could trust, and that if anyone ever truly knew who I was, they wouldn't love me. I was in a dark lonely place for a long time. Eventually, after I moved home, I bounced from treatment center to treatment center and was unable to stay sober or get my life together. I started crashing cars and selling more drugs and getting into more trouble with the law and would fail my drug tests for my probation.

I was unable to truly give up until I hit rock bottom. I had become suicidal and began to swallow handfuls of pills, and when I met with my parole officer she told me if I didn't get my life together she would throw me in jail. At that point I decided to give sobriety a shot. I had nothing left to lose, and I was unsure of how long it would last. I was an emotional train wreck when I got sober and was insanely delusional and fought and struggled to stay sober. In order to stay sober, I needed to go to inpatient, and there I went.

At first, I just wanted to stay sober until my probation ended, but at this treatment center something changed. I told myself that I was miserable, so why not give this a full shot. I had nothing left to lose. A spark of willingness ended up changing my life. I experienced a spiritual awakening there and realized that everything I wanted I could get by getting sober. I was able to let my guard down and let people love me for the real me. I was able to build real friendships with people who cared passionately about each other. I was able to finally be happy and be myself, and by the grace of God, the 12 steps, and the love that's gotten me here, I have stayed sober ever since.

"The best way out is always through."
Robert Frost

LEAP OF FAITH

By Anonymous

Growing up, I lived a normal life and most things came easily to me. In fact, I stood out to many parents, family members, and teachers, who saw potential for me to do great things in my life. I started experimenting with drugs and alcohol when I was around fifteen. At the beginning, I never paid any consequences. I kept good grades and my good reputation.

Throughout the next two years, my usage progressed and became out of control. Parents that used to love me no longer wanted their kids to hang out with me, I stopped playing sports, and I could not seem to find any enjoyment in life without using substances. Eventually, I realized I was ruining my life and took a leap of faith and asked my mom for help.

March 1, 2017 was the day my life changed. I got on a plane to California headed for a residential inpatient treatment center. Throughout my time there, I met many people who showed me what my life could look like if I worked towards my sobriety. After a month in residential treatment, I faced the real challenge. Coming home meant reentering my old environment. The hardest part was getting my phone back and seeing my old friends.

Fortunately, within a few days of returning home, I joined an outpatient program. I often tell people I would not have stayed sober coming home from residential treatment without outpatient therapy. For me, it was so important I became friends with young people that had the same goal as me, to find a better way of life. Outpatient provided me with this opportunity. For the next four months, I went to outpatient from 1:00 pm-5:00 pm every day and worked on making my life better by working the 12 steps and finding a connection with God. By the end of those four months, every aspect of my life had changed. The thing that makes outpatient therapy so successful is they allow you to go to their meetings and functions for two to three years after you finish their outpatient program.

I have stayed extremely involved in the program in the year and a half since I have been out of outpatient. I made it my responsibility to help people that are newly sober. I lead meetings, set up and cleaned for functions, and have other kids that I sponsor and I walk through the 12 steps. I have turned into a leader and am no longer afraid to take risks. I have made friends better than I could have ever asked for. My favorite part about the program is it provides me an opportunity to help people and give back, which in return makes me feel happy and fulfilled. I truly believe God did for me what I could not do for myself.

Today marks almost two years of sobriety and I can proudly say every aspect of my life has changed for the better. I no longer regret the mistakes I have made and instead see them as necessary pieces for me to make a change in my life. I feel like I got my life back and have gotten back the opportunities I thought I ruined for myself.

"One day at a time."

PART OF A PACK

By Maddie

I believe I am one in a pack. I am one of many college students who have nearly self-destructed. So many students struggle with depression, anxiety, bipolar disorder, and alcoholism. But my story is a little different. Nothing negative happened to me, my circumstances did not "create" me. I could describe my perfect childhood, my perfect family, and my perfect privilege, but they would only stand in contrast to my near self-destruction. Through this essay, I will describe three personal experiences and what they have collectively taught me.

As a sophomore in high school, I discovered the power of alcohol and the way it made me feel. It was as though something clicked. The whole world made sense, and I could not imagine life without it. My first experience drinking alcohol was on a Tuesday night. It was not supposed to be a "let's get drunk and see what happens" night, but that is what it became. I was going to see Kesha in concert with some friends and we were drinking alcohol. I was dressed for the theme: tutu, glitter, and all. It was supposed to be the perfect night. However, all I could recall the next day was being taken out on an ambulance stretcher. I learned that night I could not handle my liquor.

But that didn't stop me.

In the summer of 2015, I joined a group traveling abroad through Greece. It was a dream: the sights, the smells, the people. It was unbelievably beautiful. I wanted to travel endlessly in Greece. Then, nightmare struck. My grandfather passed away back at home. I was very close with my grandfather. He drove me to school every morning. He brought me cookies to lunch just to make me smile. While I was in Greece, he passed away. It was an incomprehensible situation: the beauty of the Greek landscape alongside my terrible grief.

I will always have regrets: missing his passing; not appreciating the beauty around me; and drinking excessively to ease the pain. If only I would have gone home. If only I would have enjoyed my trip more. If only I would have resisted all the alcohol. If only I learned my lesson.

My final drinking incident was on an Alabama game day. My last memory was at 10 am taking a shot of vodka straight from the bottle. I woke up in the ICU later that day and was told my blood alcohol content (BAC) upon arrival was 0.45. A BAC of 0.40 and above is considered life threatening due to suppression of vital life functions. When I woke up, the doctor was relieved that I had survived. He said he had seen others with a lower BAC die. And I was not even hungover.

Imagine getting a phone call from an emergency room physician to tell you, "Your daughter might not make it through the night. How fast can you get here?" This was the call my mother received on that Alabama game day. She was seven hundred miles away, helpless and scared. When I was adequately coherent, I had to call her. I survived. My mother's voice, I cannot begin to tell you the pain she felt.

That moment is when I knew I had to change my life. I could not keep living like this, or better yet, die like this at only twenty-one. I took a year off from school to attend an alcohol rehabilitation program in Minnesota. I learned how to help myself. I learned I am not alone. I learned life was worth living. I learned I am worth living for. I learned to live one day at a time. I believe I am not alone. I am one of many who need help to stop their own destruction. I met other people like me. I became part of a pack.

"When everything seems to be going against you, remember that the airplane takes off against the wind, not with it." Henry Ford

DOPE HOUSE

By Ray

I had a pretty normal childhood. My parents were always there for me and gave me anything I wanted and more. I was close with my two older sisters and enjoyed playing football, soccer, lacrosse, baseball, and skateboarding. I had a great family and a good upbringing.

My first experience with alcohol was when I was 12 or 13 - I can't really remember. I was with some buddies, and we drank my parents' Canadian Mist whiskey. My friends both threw up, but I didn't. I remember I didn't like the taste and the feeling was cool but not all that cool. I remember thinking that I really wanted to smoke weed and that it would be awesome. I started smoking weed at 13 and never stopped. I smoked all day, every day. I wanted to feel something different, and I associated drugs with being cool and a badass. I wanted to be cool and a badass.

Getting high changed around age 15 or 16. I started doing different drugs, selling them, and making money. At that time, I also started going down to Detroit and partying with an older crowd. Once I started taking and selling Ecstasy, acid, mushrooms, Vicodin, and Xanax, I lost interest in school and my sports. Eventually I got really heavy into opiates. The parties kind of died down, and I had a lot of lonely nights doing a lot of pills - which eventually led to heroin.

I started to realize I had a problem at 16 when I got arrested. Over and over, I kept getting arrested. The money and mental anguish took a toll on my family. Later in my drug use I was stealing from my parents, other family members, and all of my friends. I lied to everyone about everything. My parents witnessed me overdose twice and have five Xanax withdrawal seizures. I took all of my family and close friends into hell with me - something that weighed on me and still does. I saw what I was doing to my family and how I was killing them all, but I couldn't stop getting high and thought the only way out was death. So I just kept getting high and hoped it would kill me so I wouldn't hurt my family anymore.

I had a lot of low moments in addiction: I was put in jail and institutions; I experienced near death; I was homeless, living in abandoned houses in Detroit; I lived and worked in fully operational Detroit dope houses. None of it was enough to get me to stop. I had to be locked up and have my freedom taken away.

My breaking point came when I was sent to jail to wait for a 1-2 year prison sentencing with a $25,000 bail. I lay on the cement floor withdrawing from heroin, crack cocaine, and Xanax. Fifty-two men shared the 25-person capacity cell with me. The cell lights were on 24/7, and we had two toilets, one blanket, and two mice. Five days in that cell made me realize I needed to make a serious change. I wanted to do whatever I could to stay out of prison and better my life.

The judge gave me a chance at rehabilitation. After three months in jail, I got to go to rehab in Michigan. I was there for 77 days. I got into Alcoholics Anonymous and had a spiritual experience and an awakening. I realized my primary purpose was to stay sober and to help others do the same. That's why I stay - because recovery and sobriety have given me a chance at life and a chance to change my life and my family's lives. I've also been given the chance to help others get the same freedom and second chances I've been given.

I've learned too much to write down in words. It can all be summed up by just being kind and tolerant of others. I try every day to be less and less selfish, self-centered, dishonest, and fearful. I work the 12 steps with my sponsor and help people I sponsor do the same. Helping other people in recovery or not in recovery - those are the highest points of my own recovery and where I get the most joy. Now I say I'm going to do something, and I do it! I'm able to look both of my parents in the eyes and hear them tell me they love me and are proud of me. I also have a great social life. I have lots of friends and a great job. Currently, I'm working toward my goal of going to art school and pursuing fashion design. None of this would be possible if I hadn't gotten sober and stayed in recovery.

"Be patient. Nothing happens overnight, but it is really worth it over time." Ray C.

A CROOKED PICTURE

By Samuel

I started drinking so young. Alcohol was something that I always wanted and aspired to partake in. In my family, the adults weren't alcoholics, but alcohol was part of our holiday ceremonies and family functions. I just wanted to be part of all those smiles and loud laughter. However, I would say that before I started drinking, I was a quiet person who loved to read fantasy novels and was adjusted to life accordingly for my age.

I would have to say the first time I had alcohol was when I stole a beer from the fridge. I was really young. I couldn't tell you exactly when this was, but I do remember hiding behind the couch and drinking part of it. I think the first time I actually got drunk was around 5th grade at a friend's house. My friend jokingly asked his mom if we could have some beers and she said yes. From then on we were allowed to party at his house as long as we didn't tell anyone or go anywhere outside the property.

I wanted to drink alcohol because I thought it was cool and previously had small amounts at family functions. I loved the warm feeling of it absorbing into my body and the immediate sense of the world righting itself like a crooked picture going level. From then on, I was hooked. I still sometimes get cravings for it.

Alcohol is my drug of choice, but I most certainly have dabbled in different substances. I was always very fond of weed and would never buy painkillers, but if I had them, I would most certainly take them. I was also part of the whole spice craze (when that was still legal) because I could just go to the smoke shop and buy it...No lazy drug dealer required. Otherwise I did mushrooms, salvia, and cocaine on just a few occasions.

My using really started to change when everyone else graduated from college. I could barely pass my classes. Eventually I started to fail them. It also started to change when getting black out drunk was not something cool anymore. I even started having a hard time doing anything without alcohol. If the event/function was going to be cool, then it had better have a lot of alcohol. It became depressing when I started drinking alone. I didn't want to get wasted around other people because I was afraid of what I would do. I always knew that I was guaranteed to throw up and continue drinking till I fell over and passed out.

Eventually, I was kicked out of college, hurt my relationship with my girlfriend by lying, and started to have serious health effects. I actually had to get a hip replacement and had gout...in my 20's. That was a rough pill to swallow. I began to realize that I was causing others harm, but by the time I truly understood this, I was deep into addiction. At that time I couldn't stop alone. When I was left to my own devices then I got drunk. The breaking point for me was realizing that if I wanted to keep anything that I had in my life, I had to get sober. My family was no longer willing to help me, my girlfriend was about to leave me, and my health was getting worse. I just remember waking up in the morning determined not to drink, and by 10:30 I was heading out to buy vodka on my credit card telling myself I would be able to stay sober tomorrow.

I had two big lows that led to my sobriety. The first one was when my family called me to tell me they had taken off work to go to my college graduation. I was most certainly not going to graduate. I hadn't even been to a class in around eight months, and my "graduation" was only a week away when they called me. The second one was when I was in detox and tried to send a letter. I was told that I could have no outside contact with the world unless I was leaving. I truly felt alone then, and all I could think about was how did I get to be this broken. I cried, and then from there on I have been in recovery.

I stay in recovery because I want more out of life than just getting drunk. There was a time when drinking was fun, but those days have long since passed. I no longer get the solace and comfort out of drinking that I once did. I remain in recovery so that I can do the things that I think any decent person should be doing.

Every day is not the same. Some days will be easy and some will be hard. It's because of this that we must take it one day at a time. We cannot say, "There is no light at the end of the tunnel," nor should we rest on our laurels, and get comfortable with time sober. I've learned that I get out of recovery what I put into it.

Often in meetings I feel like I finally belong somewhere, and there are people who understand what it's like to be me. I no longer have this terminal case of being unique and a dissatisfied human being. Oh sure, I have repaired relationships and will graduate in one month with my bachelors degree, but it's belonging to a group of people and letting go of my troubles that I love the most. Recovery has repaired my relationship with my girlfriend, and I'll finally be graduating college, eight years after finishing high school. I'm actually planning on proposing soon after the snow starts this winter. I've also gained some semblance of spirituality and the ability to let the universe have its way in most matters.

"Take it slow. Sobriety time doesn't give you any kind of immunity, and, in fact, it can cause you to relapse because the memories of pain have become so distant. I would recommend that you find others to connect with. We are social creatures who want connections. We just used to make them with alcohol and drugs" Samuel

SAD, STUCK AND SICK

By S. C.

I had a hard time making friends and was often bullied in elementary school. In middle and high school there was some bullying, but I also had some friends. I frequently felt like I was not really a part of any particular group, even though I did have some friends. I had a hard time feeling like I truly belonged anywhere. My childhood was OK, but there was some domestic violence that I witnessed and was subjected to when I was very young. We also moved around a lot before I was 6. After my parents got divorced when I was 6, we settled into a small town, and that's where the feelings of alienation started.

I had sips of alcohol every so often throughout my childhood. The earliest that I recall is when we lived in Ecuador and were part of the Hash House Harriers running group – a British ex-pat cross country/outdoors group – and after one run in particular, we all had a picnic that included a kids' "drinking contest" of Sprite mixed with beer. I was a participant at 6 years old. I have no idea how much beer was actually mixed in the Sprite. I don't remember it tasting that bad, so it must have been mostly Sprite. I remember some Kahlua with milk (again, mostly milk) when I was about 10. I felt a definite effect from alcohol for the first time when I was 16 and had some very strong beer in Lithuania with a friend and her family, again under parental supervision. When I went back to Sweden after visiting with my friend's family, that's when I started getting drunk with friends as often as we could. We couldn't do it often, but every month or every couple of months we would drink. I always got as drunk as I possibly could as quickly as I possibly could, so long as I was drinking with no parental supervision.

I had many first times trying alcohol throughout my childhood, and most of those times it was because a parent was giving it to me and telling me it was OK because it was a special occasion. By the time I was 20, I was realizing that I didn't drink the way other people drank. I wanted to do it every day. I wanted to get very, very drunk every time. I did not want to deal with the consequences – embarrassment, assault, and drunk driving – and so I felt that doing it at home would be the safest. I'd maybe have a drink or two in public, but I wouldn't drink the way I wanted to until I got home. I definitely slipped up a lot, but that was at least how I tried to manage things. Once I was home, I could really drink the way I wanted to drink.

My drinking started affecting my life and my family. The biggest thing is that I was never really able to be open or connect to other people. I couldn't let anyone in. If I let anyone see the real me, they'd see how bad the drinking was, and I was so ashamed and so afraid of that happening. That meant I was also distant from my family. But I didn't really see it as harming them at the time. I saw it as only hurting myself. I saw my isolation as protecting others, but of course it hurt people who either wanted to be close or had been close to me but couldn't be any longer.

I didn't have a big dramatic rock bottom. I just got to a point in my drinking where I was doing it every day, and the amount of time that I could go without drinking during the day – to go to school and work – that time kept getting shorter and shorter. I was also getting more frequent panic attacks. There was no big blowup moment, though. Eventually, my mom had a gentle confrontation with me about my drinking over the phone. She basically just said that if I wanted help for my drinking problem that she and my stepdad would be there.

I'm in a recovery program because I just never want to be that sad and that stuck and that sick ever again. I keep coming back to the program because I really like my life now, and I want to keep what I have, and, in order to do that, I have to stay well. I have to "feed" my recovery every day, every week. It looks different today than it did when I first found recovery, and that's good, but I still must "feed" my recovery regularly. I don't just get to check out. It's just like exercising. I'll quickly become unwell and unhealthy if I totally stop exercising. It's OK if that exercise gets easier over time, but I must still do it to maintain. Recovery is no different.

I'm a huge over-achiever. I used to use my achievements – school and work performance – as a façade to hide my addiction. The biggest thing I've had to learn in recovery is that it's OK to have hopes and dreams and aspirations, as long as I know they're not going to fix me. I do a lot today, but it's qualitatively very different than what it used to look like when I'd do a lot and juggle a lot of different activities. Today I'm not doing it because I think it's going to mean that I'm OK. I can only become OK on the inside first, separately. And when I'm OK on the inside, then I've got the capacity to actually juggle all the stuff that I want to do in my big, full, fun life.

Getting married has definitely been the biggest proof of my radical change in recovery. I couldn't maintain an acquaintanceship, let alone a long-term relationship, and so becoming someone who can truly let someone into my life in this way is huge. It's the ultimate sign that I have fundamentally changed as a person.

Today I have a career that is totally different than what I expected, and it has far surpassed my wildest dreams. My dream of being a published author by the time I'm 30 has also come true – just not in the way I wanted it to when I was a kid. I was thinking I'd be a novelist, but instead I'm working on my 2nd academic book chapter – but, hey, I did achieve that dream, just in a different way! I've got a wonderful husband, 3 adorable and loving pets, and am looking forward to building my family and my future.

"It gets better, it gets easier, and it leads to things that you just can't even imagine right now because our imaginations are limited by addiction." S. C.

BROKEN GLASS EVERYWHERE:

A COUNTER-CULTURAL DILEMMA

By Matt

By the grace of God.

By the grace of God, I am sitting here today writing this. By the grace of God, I have a successful career and education and wonderful relationships with my family. By the grace of God I have been set free.

Some of you reading this may be in a difficult situation, contemplating many things and wondering what lies ahead on your path called life. Rest assured, I was in your shoes one day. I was raised in a loving family in the suburbs of a large city. My upbringing was probably not unlike others; we weren't rich by any means, but my brothers and sisters and I had what we needed. More importantly than material possessions, we had love for each other and were close as a family. From a young age I always wanted to stick out. I wanted to be noticed. I was the class clown. I guess I started to look for acceptance from other people and began to assess my personal value on what others' perceptions were of me.

I got into middle school and remember hearing some rumors that some of my friends were smoking weed. I was always told that drugs were bad, but there was something intriguing there. It was different; it was edgy, and it would allow me to stand out and form a certain reputation with my peers. (I wouldn't really learn till many years later that the reputation of a druggie was not a very cool thing). Through middle school and into my freshman year of high school, I really took to the weed thing. It helped form some of my identity and created a sense of community and belonging with others. I was finding some of that acceptance I had been subconsciously looking for. I guess I started to notice that I was a little different from my friends at this point. We would have a weekend of partying, and instead of going home like everyone else I would be looking to score a little bit more weed or drugs for the coming week. (Hey, it's great on the weekends, right? A little bit during the week wouldn't hurt either). I also noticed the willingness and desire to move on from weed to various other harder drugs, which was also different from many of my friends.

It was around this time that I started to have a few consequences as a result of my using. My mom started to catch on to what was going on and was not pleased to say the least. There were also a few incidents at school when I was intoxicated on prescription pills and consequences ensued. I think my parents were at a loss of what to do, so they decided to send me to The Right Step, a 30-day inpatient treatment center in Houston TX. I was 14 years old. This experience was difficult; I was uprooted from my life, family, and friends and placed in a foreign setting. This is where I started to learn about recovery and the 12-steps. Unfortunately, I met a lot of different people in that place and learned a lot about other drugs as well. We were young, and I don't think any of us were particularly ready to get sober or truly understood the principles of recovery. I realize now the phenomenon at play there: we simply had not had enough consequences in our lives to realize the severity and dire nature of this disease.

I left there and returned to school. I returned to my old way of life, but something was a bit different at this point. My disease had progressed a little bit. It's like rehab had set me further down the road in my addiction. To anyone reading this, I'm sure you have heard that your addiction does not take any breaks. If you are attending a treatment center or group, and you decide to go back out, rest assured, your disease has been doing pushups waiting for you to return. A scary thought? Yes, but it's true and a warning about the dire nature of this disease. I am 31 years old now; I started on the road to recovery at 14. I wouldn't get sober till 25. I got a phone call from a friend just last week. Another one of our friends from our treatment program has passed away - an overdose. It was not the first and certainly won't be the last. It makes me so grateful to God that I was able to come out of that, and you can too.

After that first attempt at rehab, I continued using and ended up going back a few months later. I continued using and ended up at another place a few months after that. From the ages 14-18, I believe I was admitted to 8 different hospitals, rehabs, and wilderness programs. I also was a part of an outpatient group, which many of you reading this may be in. Recovery groups are an interesting thing in high school. You are young and not sure what you really want yet in life, and you are trying to stay sober, which is counter-cultural. While your "normal" friends from school are going to parties, dating, and living a seemingly normal life, you have to attend these groups for "troubled" kids. I'm not going to lie; it was very difficult for me. I went from having lots of friends and being a big part of my high school community to being constantly sent here or there, to different groups and schools, and this kind of became my reputation. I lost track of many of my "normal" friends and became isolated in a world of meager attempts at recovery and an ever-growing desire to continue using, using harder drugs.

When I was 17 years old, one night I took a bunch of crystal meth and Xanax. I ended up in the emergency room, and I almost died. I remember seeing angels in my room. I still think about that night today and wonder why my life was spared. Why was my life spared and some of my friends' lives were not? Well, now 15 years later and 6 years sober, it's beginning to make more sense. I am here to give myself back to others, to people like you, to try and make a small difference in people's lives, to give hope that there is a chance.

After I turned 18, I was able to go to college. I was actually able to stay off the hard stuff for a few years and I made some decent grades. My addiction was still ever present, but I wasn't in a position to purchase the harder drugs and managed my addiction with weed, alcohol and pills here and there. My junior year I had a friend I used with sometimes, and he introduced me to his doctor, an elderly man who would prescribe almost anything. It was at this point where my addiction revved up again. I was able to graduate college somehow, in spite of spiraling back into addiction. I was taking pain medication, stimulants, benzodiazepines, and muscle relaxers legally all in the name of "healthcare". After getting out of school I had less to keep me centered, and I began to start to seek out heavy drugs again. Things spiraled and I found myself in another treatment center, then another halfway house. Upon getting out, I moved in with a girlfriend, and after a period of sobriety, went back to heavy using.

It was around this time that loved ones began to give me ultimatums, and who would blame them? For 10 years I had been a tornado in their lives...breaking glass everywhere I went.

After some heavy using and being kicked out of my girlfriend's house, as well as my parents' house, I was at my wits end - the end of the road. I considered suicide, although somewhere deep down I knew I wanted to live. It was around that time where I cried out for help. Everything I ever knew and loved was gone, I had nothing left. I was bankrupt, physically, mentally, emotionally, and spiritually. I was given one last opportunity to go into a local detox, with the understanding that I would be moving out of state to a halfway house after discharge. I agreed to this as I had nothing left and was finally starting to accept in my mind that it was serious this time...and that it may be my last chance. After detox I moved from Texas to Florida. I didn't know anyone, had no money, just a small bag of clothes. It was a humbling experience. I remember I was finally able to get a bike to ride around. One day I was riding back from the grocery store, with the grocery bags looped around the handlebars. I hit a pothole and the groceries and bike went flying. As I lay on the pavement in that Florida sun, I realized something: I had nothing, I was at my bottom, and no one was going to help me out. I had to make a decision once and for all to make a better life for myself.

I started attending meetings again in Florida, but it was different this time. I wanted to be there, and I wanted to learn. I remember I had a sponsor who gave me a prayer and told me to get on my knees every morning and talk to God. I hadn't been to church or prayed in years...I wasn't even sure who God was anymore. But out of sheer obedience, I did it. The funniest thing started to happen - not instantly - it took a few weeks, but I started to feel a little better. I started to feel a little relief and encouragement. I began to incorporate God more and more into my life, and things continued to change for the better. I was more hopeful for the future. It was during this time where I believe I started to have a spiritual awakening. My old addictive ways of thinking started to abate a little, my mind and spirit were beginning to heal.

After things started to stabilize, I went down to the local Navy recruiting office. I had always wanted to join the service, and felt I was being pulled strongly in that direction. I raised my right hand and enlisted in the Navy as a medic. I went to boot camp with 7 months clean. The military was an amazing experience. It was the bridge that transformed me from who I was to who I am now. I was able to do a lot of cool things, from spending time in Italy to flying missions in Eastern Africa. Things were not always easy, but I hung onto the faith that I found on those difficult days in south Florida. Having gained skills and benefits in the Navy, I transitioned to the University of Texas after discharge. I am pursuing a degree in counseling, to give back a piece that was given to me.

My story is not a perfect picture of recovery. It is more like the fragments of broken glass left behind by my difficult life. But maybe it comes as an encouragement that there is not always one path to recovery, each man takes his own road. I had a lot of people help me along the way. When I was a teenager and young adult, many tried to give me advice and help, but I'm not sure how much I actually listened to it. Things simply had not gotten painful enough for me. I simply had not suffered the consequences necessary to shock my addict brain into realizing that I was in a life and death circumstance and that I was out of luck. I found God on the pavement in Florida and had a spiritual awakening. A realization that I didn't know how to run my life, that I needed God to help steer the ship.

My advice would be to heed the warnings of others and not let your life get so close to the brink. As we talked about, many people don't ever make it out, I am one of the lucky ones. But you will make your own decisions; you must walk your own path. Don't ever lose hope, and if any parents or loved ones are reading this, please don't lose hope either. My life started to change when the loved ones in my life told me that they loved me but couldn't help or be around me anymore until I was ready to help myself. But when I decided I wanted to give it one more chance, they were there. Don't ever give up. By the grace of God I now have an amazing life, amazing relationships with my loved ones, and a career where I can give back and help others.

My life has truly been transformed.

"Trust in the lord with all your heart, and lean not on your own understanding, in all your ways acknowledge him, and he will make your paths straight."

H&L

RESOURCES

To find a recovery program in your area, start with the Substance Abuse and Mental Health Services Administration. (samhsa.gov/find-help/national-helpline) (800) 662-4357

Programs in Kansas and Missouri:

- First Call
  (816) 361-5900
  (firstcallkc.org)
- Midwest Recovery Centers
  (816) 599-7382 or (844) 597-1376
  (midwestrecoverycenters.com)

Enthusiastic Sobriety Approach Programs

- The Crossroads Program-KC metro
  Kansas City, MO
  (816) 941-9400
  (thecrossroadsprogram.com)
- The Crossroads Program-St. Louis
  Chesterfield, MO
  (636) 532-9991
- Full Circle Program
  (913) 609-0943
  (fullcircleprogram.com)

Twelve Step Programs

- Alcoholics Anonymous (aa.org)
- Narcotics Anonymous (na.org)

Made in the USA
Monee, IL
05 August 2021

75004008R00069